PAUL STRUGGLES WITH HIS CONGREGATION

HANS URS VON BALTHASAR

PAUL STRUGGLES WITH HIS CONGREGATION

The Pastoral Message of the Letters to the Corinthians

TRANSLATED BY
BRIGITTE L. BOJARSKA

IGNATIUS PRESS   SAN FRANCISCO

Title of the German original:
Paulus ringt mit seiner Gemeinde
© 1988 Johannes Verlag, Einsiedeln-Trier

Cover art: © 1991 Dick Bobnick

Cover design by Roxanne Mei Lum

© 1992 Ignatius Press, San Francisco
All rights reserved
ISBN 0-89870-386-7
Library of Congress catalogue number 91-76068
Printed in the United States of America

CONTENTS

	Introduction	7
I	The Foundations of the Teaching	11
II	The Pastor	21
III	The Congregation	39
IV	The Apostle in the Congregation	65
V	The Final Confrontation	71

INTRODUCTION

The questions people ask God and the Church change; God's answer in Christ is sufficient for all time. Even though the Church, as well as the individual priest, always has to make this answer understandable anew, its essence does not change. Paul's dramatic confrontation with the congregation of Corinth proves both: his words and actions do complete justice to the situation and yet they are timeless. Therefore his pastoral directives to this difficult congregation are still a guideline for everyone holding a Christian office.

The little sketch presented here confines itself to the Letters to the Corinthians, although parts of Galatians, Colossians, and Hebrews could have been offered to supplement the pastoral directives. The eye-to-eye confrontation with Corinth is so intense and so rich, that it includes virtually everything of importance.

We are concentrating solely on the pastoral question, thus neither a dogmatically exhaustive nor exegetically satisfying interpretation is being offered. Every expert knows how many places there are in the text where a definitive interpretation remains controversial (why should the woman wear "a sign of authority" on her head during the service "because of the angels"? [1 Cor 11:10]; should the slave strive to be free or should he rather remain in his present state? [1 Cor 7:21]). We shall not take up such questions. Nor would it greatly profit pastoral understanding to research exactly what questions the Corinthians asked Paul, which he answers in the First Letter (certainly chapters 7, 8–10, 12–14) and with what instructions and reprimands he responded to what was reported to him directly or in writing (certainly chapters 5 and 6, probably 11 as well, and surely 15).

There are several other very complicated questions that we are just as little concerned with: What took place biographically between the first and the second letters? Is either one, but especially the second, composed of several parts, and if so, where are they joined? Without going into the reasons, we want to agree with the opinion that the sequence of events was as follows. The first surviving letter (which there is no sufficient reason to divide up) was preceded by a lost, earlier letter. After this earlier letter there was a visit to Corinth which went badly, following which Paul, who had returned to Ephesus, wrote the letter "with many tears" (2 Cor 2:4) and dispatched Titus to Corinth. When Titus finally brought him back good news (2 Cor 7:6), he sent the second surviving letter, announcing his own arrival. This letter of reconciliation seems to consist of chapters 1 to 7 (6:14 to 7:1 is certainly a copyist's interpolation), while chapters 8–9 about the collection for Jerusalem (presumably two different pieces of writing) do not necessarily belong to the letter of reconciliation. Chapters 10–13, in which he settles accounts with the enemies, are quite different in character and presumably are a part of the letter "with many tears". They are extremely important for us. We will not go into the chapters about the collection in detail. We take the letters as they are presented, as inspired texts of the New Testament.

The pastoral, rather than dogmatic, orientation of this little book unfortunately does not allow us to unfold the inexhaustible theological depth of the letters, or even of the themes touched upon; these could be far more richly orchestrated by quotations from the other letters. For the theology, we must direct the reader to the numerous commentaries.

I

THE FOUNDATIONS OF THE TEACHING

Paul presents his doctrine to the congregation with power and absolute clarity—against their inclinations. Its central theme is *Cross and Resurrection*, found in the First Letter's opening and second-to-last chapters. This "gospel is veiled" (2 Cor 4:3) and is "an aroma from death to death" (2 Cor 2:16) only to one who has been "blinded" by "the god of this world" (2 Cor 4:4). But for those claiming to be "spiritual" (1 Cor 2:13), whether they want to hear it or not, "the word of the Cross" (the principle of the Cross, 1 Cor 1:18), contains the basis for all that follows, including the solution to all the congregation's problems. With full force he impresses on them that God's seeming foolishness in allowing his Son to be crucified and in the "absurdity of the preaching of the gospel" (1 Cor 1:18; 1:21ff.) flies in the face of all human wisdom; "the rulers of this age" (Caiaphas and Pilate) could not understand it (1 Cor 2:8ff.).

One has to see Paul's *message of the Cross* in its fullness: it tells us that Christ "who knew no sin" was made "to be sin on our behalf" (2 Cor 5:21); this event springs solely out of "the love of Christ" (2 Cor 5:14) and this, in turn, out of the love of God the Father, who "was in Christ reconciling the world to himself", "not reckoning their trespasses against them" (2 Cor 5:18ff.). God's will to forgive and the atonement Christ achieved form such a unity that, for Paul, there can be no talk of Christ's Cross being a punishment. Paul focuses first and foremost on the implications: by means of the Cross, we (mankind) have attained "righteousness and sanctification, and redemption" (1 Cor 1:30), yes, even "the righteousness of God" (2 Cor 5:21), and that inwardly—we have become temples of God (1 Cor 3:16) and of his Holy Spirit (1 Cor 6:19)—which means we owe absolutely everything to his loving grace (1 Cor 4:7). Through the bloody sacrifice of the Cross and the form it takes in the Church as baptism and Eucharist ("sharing in the blood of Christ" [1 Cor 10:16]) we are actually incorporated into the holiness of Christ. The entire doctrine of the Body of Christ, of which we are "individually members" (1 Cor 12:27), issues directly from the event of the Cross. Undoubtedly, it stands at the center of world history; everything that came before served as "examples" (1 Cor 10:6), all that follows is proclamation and unfolding. But the whole structure of the Church is also determined by the Cross. Its function—as we must demonstrate—is to participate in God's work in the world. Since God "has committed to us the word of reconciliation" (2 Cor 5:19), (a result of the Cross), this function is nothing other than "the ministry of reconciliation" (2 Cor 5:18), and therefore it has its special share in what took place at the Cross. But so does the congregation as a whole and each individual member of it: as they behold the Lord, all of them are to be more and more transformed into his likeness.

Jesus' Cross would remain meaningless without the *Resurrection*. This is in no way a spiritual resurrection, such as the Corinthian charismatics fancied had already happened to them; rather, it is precisely that to which the historical witnesses—Cephas, the twelve, more than five hundred brethren, James, all the apostles, and lastly Paul (1 Cor 15:5ff.)—testified, after Jesus had been three days in the grave. Something different—just an immortal soul, reincarnation and the like—is quite foreign to Paul. Christ's Resurrection is the point of the whole gospel: without it our entire faith is "worthless" (1 Cor 15:17), our dead have "perished" (1 Cor 15:18), and—demonstrating the unbreakable connection between Cross and Resurrection—"you are still in your sins"

(1 Cor 15:17). Otherwise, like the prophets, our choice could be: "Let us eat and drink, for tomorrow we die" (1 Cor 15:32; Is 22:13). It is extremely significant for Paul that there is a resurrection of the body, not at all because, based on the Old Testament, he can conceive of man only as a spirit within a body, but because Christ's truly human and crucified body is decisively important for his whole doctrine of salvation. That the resurrected body is and will be a spiritual one, spiritually "life-giving" (1 Cor 15:45), and that therefore a corruptible one cannot share in God's Kingdom of heaven, does not preclude God's already having given "us the Spirit in our hearts as a pledge" (2 Cor 1:22), as those incorporated in the risen Christ. Of course the Spirit is not given the way those so-called spiritual men of Corinth imagine, for "the spiritual is not first but the natural", the corruptible; it is only after that, that we are completely conformed to the "man from heaven", Christ (1 Cor 15:46ff.). That is why Paul describes our present life "by faith not by sight" as one not yet "at home", lived "absent from the Lord" (2 Cor 5:6–7, 9), a life that longs to be "at home with the Lord"; but in the end his preference for leaving his mortal body in order to be clothed with a heavenly one yields to his willingness to live as God pleases. Paul never reflects upon the condition "between death and resurrection" (not even in the passage 2 Cor 6:1–10).

The death and Resurrection of Christ are the source of all the dogmatic truth that still needs to be proclaimed.

First, the truth it holds about God. These letters state and even presuppose that God is a *Trinity*, open to the world, which it shelters and enfolds. This sheds light *on Christ:* his completed work on the Cross, by which he became for us "the power of God and the wisdom of God" (1 Cor 1:24), was not accomplished by a mere created being. From the very beginning he is "the Lord of glory" (1 Cor 2:8), both a name of God and the gift God has given us, which only the Spirit of God can enable us to recognize (1 Cor 2:12). We can see "the glory of God" shining forth from the face of Christ (2 Cor 4:6). It is he "through whom everything was made and through whom we live" (1 Cor 8:6). For *the Holy Spirit,* Paul sees as valid the same arguments that Basil will later use to show that the Spirit is God (without calling him that): only God can "make divine", can lead man into God's realm. The Spirit as the divine inner self-awareness, "searches ... the depths of God" (1 Cor 2:10), which "no one knows, except the Spirit of God" (1 Cor 2:11). This already makes it clear that the Spirit is not the impersonal force he is often claimed to be; nothing of that kind can be found in God. If you are "a temple of the Holy Spirit" (1 Cor 6:19), then "the Spirit of God dwells in you"

(1 Cor 3:16). The Spirit distributes God's gifts "just as he wills" (1 Cor 12:11) for where he is "there is freedom" (2 Cor 3:17). He is given to us as a pledge, signifying that we are God's children in glory (2 Cor 1:22). The Resurrection of Jesus can be proclaimed in "the spirit of faith" (2 Cor 4:13). The liturgical conclusion of the Second Letter begins by citing "The grace of the Lord Jesus Christ, and the love of God" and then cites "the fellowship of the Holy Spirit" as well (2 Cor 13:13). The latter can signify the fellowship created by the Spirit as well as participation in him; in either case he is credited with a divine work.

But if the triune God opens himself to the world in Christ's death and Resurrection, then everything Christ accomplished in the world and in history attests to man's participation in the inner life of God. There has "not entered into the heart of man, all that God has prepared for those that love him" (1 Cor 2:9; cf. Is 64:3). What is meant by this is the entire plan of salvation, which Paul will describe as the fruitful Body of Christ, composed of many members, with all its ministries and other gifts of grace. Its construction is described in trinitarian terms as "the building up of the Church" (1 Cor 14:12) through "Spirit", "Lord", and "God" (Father) (1 Cor 12:4–6). And though this Church is usually called "the Body of Christ", or "a temple of the Holy Spirit", we must not forget that neither the Spirit nor Christ ever appears as an independent power in relation to the Father. As "you belong to Christ", so "Christ belongs to God" (1 Cor 3:23); the fulfillment will come about "when he (Christ) delivers up the kingdom to God the Father . . . that God may be all in all" (1 Cor 15:24, 28). Everything belonging to this world and the Church—be it work or word or sacrament—is always finally viewed by Paul in the light of the triune God.

The third chapter will go into the details. What needs to be stressed here is the aggressive sharpness Paul uses—out of pastoral necessity—to present all the foundational dogmatic truths. He complains that he has no choice. Precisely because they imagine that they are charismatic spiritual people, the Corinthians "are still fleshly" (1 Cor 3:3) in their arrogance. Therefore the Apostle cannot speak to them "as to spiritual men", but only as to "babes in Christ" (1 Cor 3:1); he can give them only "milk to drink, not solid food", for they are "not yet able to receive it" (1 Cor 3:2). He has to drum into their heads the elementary Christian truths, the newly developed basic dogmas, which they may know in some theoretical fashion but from which they are unable to draw the most simple conclusions about Christian life, as their behavior and their whole attitude prove. But there is no other approach to understanding and mastering these than with "God's wisdom, a mysterious, a hidden wisdom . . . [which] God predestined before the ages to our glory" (1 Cor 2:7).

Though Paul is capable of taking an ironic tone in addressing the presumptuous, he never becomes bitter. He emphasizes that everything is spoken in love and because of love. But he must get rid of "the old leaven" (1 Cor 5:8), so that the Christian feast can be celebrated with *joy*. It is amazing what preeminence this joy has in all Paul's letters. Since he has taken over "the ministry of reconciliation", and this requires a feast of joy for God and mankind, he wants at any cost to bring joy—to radiate joy. "Not that we lord it over your faith, but are workers with you for your joy" (2 Cor 1:24). All that was distressing has been settled with the Corinthians in writing, so that he can take "joy" in them when he arrives, "having confidence in you all, that my joy would be the joy of you all" (2 Cor 2:3). The Apostle may seem to be sorrowful, yet he is actually "always rejoicing" (2 Cor 6:10); "finally, brethren, rejoice" (2 Cor 13:11). It is only the "cheerful giver" that "God loves" (2 Cor 9:7), and the man who holds office must, above all, be that kind of a giver.

II

THE PASTOR

1. The Work of the Church as Mission

For Paul, the origins of the Church are solely "from on high", from Christ and his commitment to us. To be a Christian is to live "in Christ", through him and for him, letting him color our whole attitude. A Christian knows that since Christ died for all men, no one is allowed to go on living for himself but for the One who draws believers together in love ("Love does not seek its own" [1 Cor 13:5]). But this most basic truth about Christ and the Church can reach the people only through the *apostles,* whom Christ chose and *sent.* Paul includes himself in their ranks: "Against my will I have a stewardship entrusted to me" (1 Cor 9:17), an office that sets him where Christ is, in the last place of all (1 Cor 4:9). But this is the place of "the herald" or "ambassador" of

God's reconciliation with the world (2 Cor 5:20), who is in fact "God's fellow worker" (1 Cor 3:9; 2 Cor 1:24) in tilling God's acre and erecting his building. Of course, this makes him only one of the "ministers through whom you became believers, each of them doing only what the Lord assigned him" (1 Cor 3:5), but building well calls for a "wise master-builder" (1 Cor 3:10) and a hardworking one at that: "His grace toward me did not prove vain; but I labored more than all of them, yet not I, but the grace of God with me" (1 Cor 15:10). This is a hard, often seemingly pitiless grace whose work demonstrates two things: we can accomplish nothing without it, but neither can it get along without a tool. And even though God makes use of several workmen (Apollos and many others besides Paul), they are in no way interchangeable; each of them was chosen as the unique and irreplaceable person he is: "I planted, Apollos watered . . ." (1 Cor 3:6).

It is significant that though the difference in rank between the Apostle and his coworkers persists even when he names them in addressing a letter ("Paul, called as an apostle of Jesus Christ and Sosthenes, our brother" [1 Cor 1:1]), Paul wants his "fellow workers" (that word again! [2 Cor 8:23]), Titus and Timothy, to be just as highly esteemed by the congregation as he is himself. When Timothy comes to Corinth, he is to be treated like the Apostle, "for he is doing the

Lord's work, as I also am. Let no one therefore despise him" (1 Cor 16:10–11). If Paul is his congregation's bishop, then his fellow workers may be designated as auxiliary bishops. The pastoral letters make it clear that they have the necessary authority (in Crete, Titus is instructed to "appoint elders in every city as I directed you" [Titus 1:5]). The Church, says Paul, is "built upon the foundation of the apostles and (New Testament) prophets" (Eph 2:20); the latter, according to 1 Corinthians 12 to 14, are those whom the Spirit authorizes as interpreters of God's word. Of course Christ remains the "foundation" or "cornerstone", but the building does not grow to be a holy temple of the Lord without the continuing assistance of the "fellow workers". "But let each man be careful *how* he builds upon it" (1 Cor 3:10). Precisely because the (fellow) workers are promoters (*auctores*) of the building, they have the right to exercise the determining influence (*auctoritas*). Despite what is sometimes claimed nowadays, there is no trace of Church democracy in Paul's writing. Instead there is *koinonia,* "fellowship" (1 Cor 1:9; 10:16; 2 Cor 13:14) based on, and called for, by Christ's love. *Koinonia* requires us to live for one another, which means being open and transparent in mutual love. This will turn out to be exactly what Paul demands of the pastoral office.

This *mutual openness,* which should banish all mistrust, is the reason why Paul has no difficulty in uniting love and obedience in the Church (2 Cor 7:15). The paradigm of this unity is Christ's obedience, even unto death; therefore the Corinthians, too, must be "obedient in all things" to the Apostle. Paul will not be able to cleanse the congregation of all the rebels' "disobedience" (*parakoē*) until it is completely on his side; not until "your obedience (*hypakoē*) is complete" can he "take captive every thought to make it obedient (*hypakoē*) to Christ" (2 Cor 10:5–6). If the congregation is to obey the office Paul holds, then his openness toward them must also display his boundless love for them. His assurances are almost gushing while his only complaint is their lack of love in return. "If I love you the more, am I to be loved the less?" (2 Cor 12:15; 6:11ff.). He not only protests his love, but proves it by being a genuine pastor; there is no other congregation for whom he did and suffered as much, completely unselfishly (as he keeps stressing [1 Cor 9; 2 Cor 11:7ff.; 12:14]). That is why—unlike "countless tutors"—he has every right to call himself their only "father", and them "my beloved children" (1 Cor 4:14ff.). Not only has he "begotten" them but he "will most gladly spend and be expended for your souls" (2 Cor 12:15).

The unity between the authority of the Church and the community of the Church finds its ultimate expression in the delicate decisions which Paul, as the pastor in charge, has to make alone but doesn't want to make without the congregation's consent. At this point two passages have to be read together. In the first, "though absent in body but . . . present in spirit", Paul has "already judged" the one who committed gross immorality: "In the name of our Lord Jesus, when you are assembled and I with you in spirit, with the power of our Lord Jesus, I have decided" to shut this man out of the Church for a time (1 Cor 5:3–5). In the second, because "you are in our hearts, even to the sharing of death and life together" (2 Cor 7:3) and because Paul's reproach caused them to repent sufficiently (2 Cor 7:9ff.), he can let the congregation take the initiative in accepting another sinner back, and then confirm their decision by agreeing with it. "You should rather forgive and comfort him, lest somehow such a one be overwhelmed by excessive sorrow. Wherefore I urge you to reaffirm your love for him . . . But whom you forgive anything, I forgive also; for indeed what I have forgiven, if I have forgiven anything, I did it for your sakes in the presence of Christ" (2 Cor 2:7–10). Both passages demonstrate the unity of the pastoral office and the congregation in the love of Christ, but in the first, the pastoral office takes the initiative while getting the congregation involved, whereas in the second, it lets the congregation take the first step; providing it is done in the love of Christ, the pastoral office will have no problem in assenting to it.

In the final analysis, the unity between the pastoral office and the congregation becomes tangible in *the pastoral office's need for the congregation's prayer,* in order to carry out its work in accordance with God's will. Paul requests this intercessory prayer in all his letters (Rom 15:30; Eph 6:19; Col 4:3; 1 Th 5:25; 2 Th 3:1; Heb 13:18), including those to the Corinthians (2 Cor 1:11). He does not seek it for his personal benefit, but so that the favor bestowed on him through the prayers of many, may cause many to give thanks (2 Cor 1:11), once again, in the spirit of community.

2. *The Dignity of the Pastoral Office*

The letter of reconciliation contains such a long discourse on the grandeur of the New Testament pastoral office (2 Cor 2:14–7:13), that it has sometimes been considered an independent composition. It does, in fact, divide Paul's account of his journey from Troas to Macedonia right in two. Paul doesn't always keep to a Greek logical format, but all the same, the passage fits into the context: he has to explain to the Corinthians how his authority is revealed. His purpose is not to distance himself from the congregation, but "that you may have an answer for those who take pride in appearance, and not in heart" (2 Cor 5:12).

The description of the pastoral office's glory accents three characteristics: it is the operation of the Holy Spirit; it is openness to God and the world; and in a paradoxical way it is participation in the suffering and Resurrection of Christ. The conclusion of each point leads to the next.

a. *The Pastoral Office in the Spirit* (2 Cor 3:1–18). The proof begins very beautifully, with the assurance that none of the apostles can become "servants of [the] new covenant" on his own, for this is a "covenant . . . of the Spirit", and only the Spirit of God can make the servants "adequate". The proof of adequacy does not, however, rest in the servant himself, but in the congregation, which is "a letter of Christ . . . known and read by all men . . . written . . . not on tablets of stone, but on tablets of human hearts". Since the pastoral office can act effectively only in the Holy Spirit, the letter is not designated as a letter of Paul, the servant, but as a letter of Christ himself. The best the bond-servant could do would be to write "with ink", but this would not be adequate for the Spirit. Thus Paul sets himself apart: first polemically, from his foes in Corinth, who came with paper "letters of recommendation" (2 Cor 3:1; 10:18); secondly from Moses and his law that was written "on tablets of stone". He does not deny Moses a certain "glory", but the law—here referred to as "the old covenant"

(3:14)—could not lead to the living Spirit; it "fades away" (3:11), is merely transitory and therefore symbolized by the veil which covers the face of Moses (Ex 34:34). Once the veil is removed, the "unveiled face" of the Christian, and of Christ himself, introduce the second characteristic mark of the pastoral office. The marvelous passage, which calls the glorified Christ "pneuma" (Spirit) and thus "liberty" (from the veil of the law), certainly applies to all of Christendom. The miracle of the newly radiating light, however—a miracle as great as the light called out of darkness at the creation of the world—is primarily placed in the heart of the one called to the office of apostle: "For God who said, 'Light shall shine out of darkness', is the One who has shone in our hearts to give the light of the knowledge of the glory of God in the face of Christ" (2 Cor 4:6). If we recognize the connection with "the lifegiving Spirit" (2 Cor 3:6), the trinitarian character of this statement about the pastoral office appears.

b. *The Manifestation of the Pastoral Office* (2 Cor 4:1–6). This shorter section is significant. The apostolic ministry commends itself by "commending ourselves to every man's conscience in the sight of God". Manifestation (*phanērosis*) clearly shows that the essence of truth is to be without a veil (*a-lētheia*). What counts is that the manifestation as well as the one witnessing to it be transparent toward God and the world. If this manifestation is still veiled and incomprehensible for some people, this is because "the god of this world has blinded" them. The manifestation is unveiled because "the glory of Christ" in "the gospel" "is the image of God". And the witness to it is unveiled because—unlike Paul's enemies, with their craftiness and furtiveness (4:2)—"we do not preach ourselves but Christ Jesus as Lord, and ourselves as your bond-servants for Jesus' sake" (4:5). Paul sees openness "to every man's conscience" as both a gift and a requirement. That is why he defends himself at length to his congregation about his travel plans. "Our word to you is not yes and no" (2 Cor 1:18). He had planned to go directly to Corinth (2 Cor 1:23), but after incidents that occurred during an intervening visit, he fell back on an earlier plan to go by way of Macedonia. He wants the congregation to know why. "To spare you" he sent Titus on ahead to bring him news in Macedonia about the mood in Corinth; this news comforted him (2 Cor 7:7). He had already rendered this kind of account in the first letter (1 Cor 16:5ff.). Paul's obligation to be open rests ultimately in Christ himself. Through Jesus, God speaks an unconditional Yes to the world, in which all (as yet unclear) promises find their Yes, meaning their answer, so that Christians can say "Amen" to the entirety of God's word (2 Cor 1:19ff.). The Corinthians ought to make up their minds to say that same "Amen" to their "father", Paul, as well. "We are made manifest [transparent] to God; and I hope that we are made manifest [transparent] also in your consciences" (2 Cor 5:11). Any kind of diplomacy is quite foreign to Paul. The only time he speaks as a "crafty fellow" who "took you in by deceit" (2 Cor 12:16), he is probably taking up a reproach leveled against him: Do they think he used any of the money that was collected for himself (2 Cor 8:20), or have those he sent "taken advantage of you"? (2 Cor 12:17). He rejects the reproof; Titus and the others "walked in the same steps" as he (12:18).

There is another aspect of his transparency which is subtle and easily misunderstood: since all, Jews and Gentiles alike, have the right to understand the gospel, the Apostle must make himself "a slave to all" (1 Cor 9:19) and "become all things to all men" (9:22). But since the gospel itself is for everyone, he was not dissembling if "to the Jews" he "became *as* a Jew", and "to those who are without law, *as* without law" (9:21). He goes on to explain: "To those who are under the law", he must appear as one who fulfills the law perfectly (as Jesus himself did), "though not being myself under the (old, superseded) law"; while "to those who are without law", he must appear "as without law, though not being without the law of God but under the law of Christ" (9:20–21). As an attitude this was quite feasible; in practice it could lead to necessary compromises (such as Timothy's circumcision) and subsequently, in view of the Jerusalemites' narrow-mindedness, to Paul's imprisonment and eventual martyrdom. Being forced to live in the midst of the tension between Jews, Jewish Christians, and pagan Christians brought him no conflict of conscience, but it did lead to the hardest possible conflicts with his environment. Here we have the transition to the final aspect of the pastoral office, which can be considered the third aspect of the entire treatise.

3. *The Pastoral Office as Imitation of Christ (2 Cor 4:7–7:13).*

The constant attack he was under, especially in Corinth, was Paul's strongest proof that his whole life consisted of being Christ's witness. His "foolish" speech, in which he boasts only of his "weaknesses", "insults", "distresses", "persecutions", and "difficulties for Christ's sake" (2 Cor 12:10), is meant as explicit proof of the authenticity of his apostolic calling. In the First Letter he had already ironically contrasted his standing "last of all, as men condemned to death", "having become a [circus] spectacle to the world, both to angels and to men" (1 Cor 4:9), and all his other suffering, right down to "having become as the scum of the world, the dregs of all things" (4:13), with the Corinthians' arrogant (1 Cor 8:1) and haughty character. "If anyone supposes that he knows anything, he has not yet known as he ought to know" (1 Cor 8:2).

All of the third part of the treatise on the Christian pastoral office is devoted to its being a following of Christ; it makes it very clear that for the Apostle, as for any Christian, following the Cross also means following the Resurrection. To put it more plainly: *Christ gives the grace to follow the Cross only because he rose again.* This creates a distance between the Lord and his servant, of which Paul is fully aware. There can be no "Paul's party" in Corinth, for "Paul was not crucified for you, was he?" (1 Cor 1:13). Thus, in this part of the discussion of the pastoral office, two things can be stated simultaneously: that "we carry about in our bodies the dying of Jesus, so that in our bodies the life of Jesus may also be revealed" (2 Cor 4:10)—God's herald says "when I am weak, then I am strong" (2 Cor 12:10)—and that "we who live are constantly being delivered over to death for Jesus' sake . . . So death works in us, but life in *you* (2 Cor 4:11–12). One who follows Jesus can also share with Jesus in suffering in place of the congregation. So the Apostle's strength in his weakness turns out to be God's strength again, after all; upon being buffeted by "a messenger of Satan", he received God's reply: "My grace is sufficient for you, for my power is perfected in weakness" (2 Cor 12:8–9). This twofold aspect of the pastoral office's suffering reaches its climax in 2 Corinthians 13:3–4. We will come back to that. The important thing here is that there is no undialectical identification with the crucified Lord in the pastoral office's imitation of Christ's suffering. Peter is crucified—but only upside down. When Paul makes the comparison: *"quasi morientes—et ecce vivimus"* ("as though dying yet behold we live" [2 Cor 6:9]), the "quasi" (as though) is the definitive word. The conclusion of the digression about the pastoral office lists all these paradoxes (2 Cor 6:4–10), "in order that the ministry (*diakonia*) be not discredited" (2 Cor 6:3). The "fool's speech" is similarly divided into two parts: the first is a heart-rending catalogue of the Apostle's sufferings, the second tells of his being mystically caught up into paradise and receiving revelations; but in closing it speaks again of suffering, "because of the surpassing greatness of the revelation, for this reason, to keep me from exalting myself" (2 Cor 12:7).

The third part of the discussion of the pastoral office concludes with another reminder that everything the Apostle suffers is "for your sakes" (2 Cor 4:15). He endures hardships undismayed, seeing all present suffering as "light" in comparison to the eternal weight of glory yet to come, in view of which complaints from him about the congregation's contempt or mistreatment cannot even arise. Here are the elements (in 2 Cor 5:1–10) that comprise Christian life: lived by faith and not by sight, longing to be at home with the Lord, but despite everything persevering here below, as long as it pleases him.

Looking over Paul's concept of the pastoral office, one is struck by the fact that it consists of two inextricably interconnected elements. The first is that Christ called and appointed him as an apostle, by means of his vision of Christ on the road to Damascus. This objective factor relieves him of any dependence on the opinions and demands of the congregation. "Am I not free? Am I not an apostle? Have I not seen Jesus our Lord?" (1 Cor 9:1) This factor is so objective, that Paul views it as actually having been forced on him by the Lord, and denies that it owes anything to his own merit (1 Cor 9:17–18). If he desires wages or merit, they must be sought elsewhere, in the fact that he took no pay for work for which he had a right to demand wages (1 Cor 9:4–15). But to prove that his calling as an apostle is authentic, he rests his case entirely on the second factor, his life, whose every aspect bears consistent witness that his claim is genuine. This is what makes him a lasting example to all who serve as priests. In exhorting his successor, Timothy, he sticks to both factors, but places more emphasis on the second. He reminds him that his consecration, by the Apostle's laying on of hands, was objective, but that in it "God has not given us a spirit of timidity, but of power and love and discipline. Therefore do not be ashamed of the testimony of our Lord, or of me, his prisoner; but join with me in suffering for the gospel according to the power of God" (2 Tim 1:6–8).

III

THE CONGREGATION

The Corinthians put questions to the pastoral office, which also received complaints about conditions in the congregation in other ways. In the First Letter, Paul deals with both questions and complaints, taking them as they come, without separating them. That will be the starting point for our discussion, but we will also draw on remarks from the Second Letter for clarification. Once again, the individual topics will not be subjected to thorough exegetical analysis; we are concerned only with what is clearly stressed. The Cross and Resurrection of Christ provide the framework for the topics as a whole—the accent on the Cross is aimed polemically at the spirit of division, while the accent on Resurrection is in answer to a question. Therefore it is not surprising that the main emphasis in all the answers and warnings to the congregation is *on the bodily,* taken in the full breadth of its biblical meaning: the crucified and resurrected Body of Christ, and the holiness of his Body's Church, stemming from the Eucharist which builds up this Body. This breadth can encompass the answers to the case of the sexual offender; the law suits; the problems of marriage and celibacy; consideration for the weak brother; celebration of the Eucharist; the spiritual gifts, centered on love, which serve to build up the Body of Christ (1 Cor 12:7); and finally the bodily Resurrection of Christ and the form of resurrected bodies. This clear emphasis shows that all questions of the Church should be approached from the Incarnation of God's Word, an incarnation which takes its meaning (capable of solving all religious questions) from the Cross and Resurrection of Christ.

1. *The Immoral Person* (*1 Cor 5; 6:12–20*)

Paul had already dealt with the question of immorality in the earlier letter (1 Cor 5:9, 11); now he has heard about the case of a Christian who is living with his father's wife. He makes a point of dealing with the case as purely a Church matter. The Corinthian environment is rife with licentiousness; it is not up to him to judge it, God will do that (5:12–13), but the congregation has to live in this atmosphere, otherwise "you would have to go out of the world" (5:10). The Church, however, is no place for libertinism, not because of universal moral principles, (although this kind of immorality "does not even exist among the Gentiles" [5:1]), but because "Christ our Passover has been sacrificed" (5:7) or, as is later more clearly stated, because "the Lord is for the body" and therefore the Christian's body is also "for the Lord" (6:13). In this mutual devotion lies true freedom, setting us free from any bondage to sexual desire. "All things are lawful for me, but not all things are profitable. All things are lawful for me, but I will not be mastered by anything" (6:12). Here is how we distinguish between the stomach, which digests the food—"God will do away with both of them"—and the body, which is destined for the Lord and to be raised up in the Lord (6:14) and therefore "is a temple of the Holy Spirit" (6:19).

This *christological-trinitarian basis for the holiness of the body* is fundamentally different from the Jewish condemnation of immorality. When Old Testament and Jewish authors set sexual immorality at the head of the list of sins, they did so mainly because they saw immorality as the chief characteristic of pagan society: turning away from Yahweh was looked on as whoring after strange gods; moreover the pagan cults usually involved cultic prostitution (cf. Num 25 to Ez 8). Paul also places this sin at the head of his lists, but now as seen from the perspective of the Incarnation and Cross of the Son of God. Only thus can we understand the astounding statement: "Every other sin that a man commits is outside the body, but the immoral man sins against his own body." The explanation follows immediately: "Or do you not know that your body is a temple of the Holy Spirit who is in you, whom you have from God, and that you are not your own? For you have been bought with a price" (6:18–20): the death of Christ. This is a trinitarian statement, for it is the Father who has paid this price, given up the Son, and granted the Holy Spirit. The doctrines about the Eucharist ("the Lord is for the body"), and the spiritual gifts by which the Spirit builds the Church body, are included here in advance. Therefore they are to "glorify the [triune] God in your body" (6:20). When Paul harks back to the word in Genesis: "The two will become one flesh", to stigmatize joining oneself to a harlot, the counterstatement, "but the one who joins himself to the Lord is one spirit with him" (6:16ff.), taken in the whole context, does not represent a contrast with the flesh. We might understand it more readily by means of the contrast repeated in 6:13–14, for there will come a time when sexual union will be "done away with", since what it produces is only mortal.

2. *The Lawsuits* (1 Cor 6:1–11)

The Apostle scolds the congregation, because those who have a case "go to law before the unrighteous, and not before the saints" (1 Cor 6:1), thus allowing themselves to be judged by heathen judges. A first contradiction in this conduct is that since "he who is spiritual appraises all things, yet he himself is appraised by no man" (1 Cor 2:15), a Christian has no business letting himself be judged at all. The passing of spiritual judgment on all things will become a reality in the last days, when the Body of Christ joins Christ in judging "the world" and "angels". Thus one might expect the Corinthians to have no difficulty in coming to an agreement about "the trivial cases" "of this life". A second contradiction lies in going to a pagan ("unjust") judge, who is particularly unsuited to settle differences within the Church. Were a judge needed, it would have to be a "wise man" in the Church.

But Paul goes further. The very fact that there are disputes is already "a defeat" for Christians, in view of the new law the Lord proclaimed in the Sermon on the Mount and himself followed at the Cross: rather than adding injustice, it is better to endure it yourself. "Why not rather be defrauded?" (6:7). The Greek concept of justice, by which the Corinthians judge, is to be replaced by the biblical one, already present in the Old

Testament and more pronounced in the New, of *"the righteousness of God"*. We received it as a gift by Christ's being made "sin on our behalf" (2 Cor 5:21), and thus at the Cross putting "to death" all enmity, alienation, and differences (cf. Eph 2:16). So this mistake of the congregation, too, is ultimately connected to the Cross and repudiated on its account. In concluding, Paul expands on this in a trinitarian sense: (in the Blood of Christ) the congregation is "washed, ... sanctified, ... justified", and gifted with "the Spirit of our God", therefore, being justified, not only can it have no inner relationship with "the unrighteous", but can itself not be unrighteous any longer (6:9–11).

3. *Marriage and Celibacy (1 Cor 7; 2 Cor 11:2)*

The long commentary on marriage and celibacy in 1 Corinthians, chapter 7 answers the congregation's questions with calm clarity. Paul begins with a general statement (7:1–7), and then goes into specific cases: unmarried persons and widows (7:8–9), married couples (7:10–11), mixed marriages (7:12–16), how to respond to God's calling (7:17–24), celibacy and being bound to the world (7:25–35), and then the widows again (7:39–40).

We cannot be concerned here with discussing each case in detail, especially since there are current attempts to reinterpret the entire chapter by shifting the emphases. There are two basic comments to make on these attempts. But first it should be pointed out that Paul (basing his position on that of Christ), clearly gives equal rights to wife and husband (7:3). The ultimate reason for this is man's self-surrender resulting from the Cross: "You are no longer your own" (6:17). In marriage, the husband has authority over his wife's body, the wife over her husband's body. Therefore she has the same right to a divorce as the husband. This would have been unthinkable for the rabbis or the Greek *stoa*.

The first comment: when Paul says: "I wish that all men were [unmarried] even as I myself am" (7:7), he sets (and maintains throughout the chapter) celibacy as something better than marriage. (This means one cannot translate it as: "I wouldn't mind if everyone were like me.") But this objective norm is immediately relativized by the next sentence: "However, each man has his own gift (*charisma*) from God, one in this manner, and another in that." The same thing applies here as will apply (in the disputed verses 7:1–24) to the concept "calling" (*klēsis*); both "charisma" and "klēsis" are to be taken *very broadly,* preferably the way 7:17a puts it: "as God has *called* each, in this manner let him walk". Thus the term "charisma" does not refer to a particular calling (to celibacy or to marriage), since the concept of a "calling" applies just as neutrally to the state God assigns to us (slave or free, circumcised or uncircumcised). This open-ended breadth is forced on us by the gospel, which calls us to specific ways of following Jesus (including leaving "wife and child"), but never includes anything like a "call to marriage". Marriage is a sacrament, and therefore a gift of grace, but it is not an alternative on a par with the calling to celibacy. Proof of this in Church history is given by calls from out of marriage to a life of celibacy (e.g., Brother Klaus and Saint Jane Frances de Chantal), but there are no calls to leave celibacy for marriage. This is in accord with Paul's objective hierarchy. It also makes it quite clear how married persons' "interests are divided" because they are engrossed in their spouses: the husband, "how he may please his wife" (7:33), the wife, "how she may please her husband" (7:34). Admittedly, Paul's argument throughout the passage hardly draws on imminent expectations: instead of "the form of this world is passing away", 7:31 should read: "the attitude of the world holds one in its grip." But it might be harder to reinterpret 7:29 (usually translated "The time is short", or "has been shortened") as a "proverb" (cf. Rom 13:11; 1 Pet 4:7) and to isolate from it the section that inwardly subordinates worldly kinds of behavior and demands distancing oneself from them ("those who weep as though they did not weep", etc.). This kind of demand need have nothing to do with imminent expectations.

Now the second comment: there has to be justification for the continual invitation to prefer celibacy to marriage or remarriage, or at least to consider it as a possibility. If Paul fails to give his own reason (here), he does so unmistakably in 7:34: "An unmarried woman or a virgin is anxious about the things of the Lord, so that she may be holy in both body and spirit." The word "things" is not in the text, but "of the Lord" certainly refers primarily to the Lord himself, here repeating the idea of "joining [one]self to the Lord" (6:17). This gives rise to a loftier analogy to marriage, as shown by a passage from the Second Letter: "I am jealous for you with a godly jealousy; for I betrothed you to one husband, that to Christ I might present you as a pure virgin" (2 Cor 11:2). Since he refers to the entire congregation as a virgin who is to belong to the Lord, this cannot be considered a "counsel" such as might be addressed to an individual person, and this is precisely why the objectively higher value of celibacy, in Paul's theology, is understandable without any gnostic devaluation of marriage. The final explication of this theology will come in the fifth chapter of the Letter to the Ephesians where the sexual union of man and wife, which makes them "become one flesh", is to be an image of the marriage bond between Christ and his Church.

4. *The Strong Person and His Weaker Brother* (*1 Cor 8:1–11:1*)

Just as the instructions about marriage and celibacy were painstakingly detailed and varied, so are the ones that follow about Christian freedom to eat meat that has been previously offered to a "god". First a distinction must be made between two different situations: participating in a sacrificial meal at a heathen temple, and partaking of a meal at the home of a heathen acquaintance, where meat is served that had a sacrificial ceremony performed on it at the market.

"*Knowledge* puffs up, but *love* edifies" (1 Cor 8:1). Knowledge that the heathen idols are nothing and that therefore the ceremonies in their honor mean nothing does not constitute an absolute Christian norm. No matter how completely justified our knowledge feels to us, that does not mean it is justified before God: "But if anyone loves God, he is known by him" (the only absolute One) and accepted (8:3). But to love God is to love one's neighbor, and therefore also to be considerate of the weaker brother, who in his spiritual narrow-mindedness could interpret my freedom as libertinism. "For through your knowledge he who is weak is ruined, the brother for whose sake Christ died. And thus, by sinning against the brethren and wounding their conscience when it is weak, you sin against Christ. Therefore, if food causes my brother to stumble, I will never eat meat again" (8:11–13).

Throughout an entire chapter (9:1–27), the Apostle gives himself as an example of this Christian ability to make sacrifices. As a true apostle who has seen Christ, he would have the right to let the congregation support him as they do others, but out of consideration for the congregation he has made no use of this right (9:12–15). He used his freedom to make himself everyone's slave (9:19) and made himself weak especially for the weak (9:22). He is in dead earnest about his renunciation (9:24–27). And seeking still another way to shake the assertive confidence of the strong, supposedly spiritual Corinthians, he draws on the Old Covenant: the generation in the wilderness could have deluded themselves with a sense of security as God's chosen people, "nevertheless, with most of them God was not well pleased" (10:5). They became idolaters and engaged in whoring (this remark points back at the case of the immoral brother and ahead to things still to be said); they tested Christ, the "spiritual rock which followed them" (10:4). Here is a warning to the strong: Beware of presumptuous freedom.

Then these same strong men meet with a new, unexpected turnabout, specifically relating to the sacrificial meals in pagan temples (10:14–22). To demonstrate the danger of participating in them, the Apostle takes three steps: from the pagan sacrificial meal, to that of the Jews, and from thence to the Christian one, which signifies partaking of the "Blood of Christ" in one cup, and partaking of "the one Body" of Christ in one bread. If we retrace these three steps backward, then first the Christian meal was "communion" (*koinonia*) with the Body and Blood of Christ, next the Old Testament sacrificial meal was also "sharing" in the sacrifices at the altar (10:18), and now the pagan meal really does appear in a different light. Paul again asserts that the meat sacrificed to idols is nothing, and the idols are nothing. But behind these empty things lies the demonic. Because the gentiles do not sacrifice to the true God, they sacrifice to demons; "and I do not want you to become sharers in demons" (10:20). "Or do we provoke the Lord to jealousy? We are not stronger than he, are we?" (10:22). This last sentence in effect equates arrogance, that considers itself enlightened, with the demonic. Such arrogance defies the Lord; to "put the Lord your God to the test" is for Israel (Dt 6:16) what sin, as such, is for Jesus (Mt 4:7).

Lastly, Paul comes back to considerate love for the weaker brother (10:23–11:1). Our own conscience—no matter how knowledgeable—is not the decisive factor, but rather "the other man's" (10:29). Giving "no offense" to anyone is more important than my strong conscience. Again Paul sets his own life as an example for the others to follow. "Be imitators of me [in this], just as I also am of Christ" (11:1), who gave himself on the Cross for others.

5. *The Worship Service (1 Cor 11–14)*

Everything that Paul still has to criticize, before he gets to the chapter on the Resurrection, concerns the worship service in Corinth. There are *three serious faults:* (1) lack of decorum (1 Cor 11:2–16); (2) lack of consideration for others, which is connected to the lack of reverence for the Eucharist (11:17–34); and (3) lack of order (1 Cor 12–14).

The first point gives Paul occasion to speak about the position of women, not only in the liturgy, but in the larger context of salvation. The second has preserved for us what is probably the oldest liturgical text for the Eucharist. The third and longest deals with the Corinthians' spiritual gifts and has the great "Hymn of Love" as its middle chapter; it is also aimed at clearing up problems with the divine service, as the concluding chapter (14) indicates. Only when we take these three points together does the structure of the First Letter as a whole become clear. The theme of the body is significant throughout—the Cross and the chapter on the Resurrection require it. This topic is already clear in the section on decorum (the difference between the sexes, long and short hair); it becomes obvious in the part about the Eucharist ("This is my body, which is for you" [11:24]). And it is by reference to the Church, as the Body of Christ, that the problem of spiritual gifts will be addressed and resolved—in the face of the Corinthian mentality.

a. *Decorum.* The whole question raised by the woman having her head covered during the worship service, which Paul expanded into a theology of the sexes that is often taken amiss, is basically concerned with maintaining decorum. This is important in every period of Church history, even when customs change. No matter how you look at it, there is nothing out-of-date in this section.

Among the Jews and Jewish Christians, but frequently in Hellenistic areas as well, especially in congregations of gentile Christians founded by Jewish Christian missionaries, it was considered indecent for women to have their hair uncovered, especially during worship. Certainly one reason why Paul insisted on holding to this traditional custom (11:2) is that setting themselves above this tradition was a mark of spiritual emancipation for the "enlightened" charismatics (the party "of Christ" [1:12]).

Paul is not here forbidding women to pray or speak prophetically during the liturgy (out loud [11:5]), as long as they maintain decorum. Therefore the contradictory prohibition (in 1 Cor 14:33b–36) must be regarded as a later interpolation, even though it appears in all the old manuscripts. The questionable composition of the Second Letter indicates how much editors contributed to genuine Pauline letters.

Paul's argument for his demand goes in steps, but the steps overlap. He appeals to a natural sense of decency: "Does not even nature (*physis*) herself teach you?" (11:14). This is in regard to short hair for men and long hair for women, which seems to lead naturally to the woman covering her hair. The same opinion was already put forth in 11:4–6, mainly on Old Testament grounds (11:7–9), but these apply to the New Testament order (11:3) as well. The Old Testament argument (Gen 2:18–24)—woman created from the man (1 Cor 11:8) and for the man (11:9)—is laid out in broad lines, but when it is carried over into the sphere of the New Testament, we see it from two viewpoints, just as in the more detailed exposition in Ephesians 5.

The first viewpoint is not really based on the Old Testament: "Christ is the head of every man, and the man is the head of a woman, and God is the head of Christ." The final justification for this is no longer that Eve originated from Adam, but that the Church originated from Christ, who therefore remains her Head; this makes it impossible for the Church to have the same relationship to Christ as he has to her. But the woman's subordination to the man, that this point of view demands, is linked to the requirement that the husband gives himself up to his wife with perfect love just as Christ did for the Church (Eph 5:25). Throughout, the gospel teaches that the leader is to behave like a servant (Lk 22:26ff.).

The second viewpoint, which concludes Paul's theological discussion, seems to contradict the first in stressing the equal rights and equal dignity of the sexes, as did chapter 7: "However, in the Lord, neither is woman independent of man, nor is man independent of woman. For as the woman originates from the man, so also the man has his birth through the woman, and all things originate from God" (11:11–12). The Genesis version (the woman from the man) is supplemented by the customary order of the sexes (the man from the woman), to which Christ as man also submits. At this point a Mariology is needed, which could not yet be written in Paul's time, as an equivalent counterbalance to the paradise story. It is inchoately implied in Paul's designation of the Church as "immaculata" (Eph 5:27).

b. *Reverence.* The wealthy persons' lack of consideration for the poorer ones at the *agape meal,* which introduced the celebration of *the Eucharist,* and the failure truly to grasp Christ's real presence in the *Eucharist* itself, are both examples of a lack of reverence. The initial reproach about divisions in the congregation is repeated here (Paul speaks of *schismata* and *hairēseis,* both in the same sense [11:18–19]). This is followed by the significant statement: "There must also be factions among you, in order that those who are approved may have become evident among you" (11:19). The fundamental division of God's people was deliberately brought about by Jesus himself; (he does not bring "peace on earth . . . but rather division" [Lk 12:51]). He requires a Yes or a No as response. Paul presents an alternative that has weighty consequences—"approved" or "unapproved"—which will play the decisive role in his final confrontation with the congregation (2 Cor 13). This "must" (in 11:19) ultimately remains hidden in the mystery of God, who strives for final unity, which he wants to achieve and which can be achieved only through decision and hence through separation.

The abuses at the agape meals are construed as contempt for "the church of God" (22), because the well-to-do are selfishly concerned with satisfying their own hunger, and cast "shame" on poorer people, who have to come later. This interpretation shows that the greatest problem is the church's lack of love, and it is the standard by which all the mistakes they are accused of in the rest of the passage are measured.

The lack of reverence is striking in view of the solemn words Paul used in reporting how Jesus instituted the Eucharist as an unalterable tradition (11:23–26). The strongest emphases are on "my body, which is for you", "the new covenant in my blood", and "do this in remembrance of me". So first there is Jesus' total offering of himself to the congregation, then this sacrifice as something completely new, in contrast to the former covenant—the Blood that is shed is not that of another but his own—and finally the act required of the Church, to bring continually into the present time the sacrifice that was made once and for all. Paul strongly emphasizes this last point in verse 26: each time the Church carries out this act "you proclaim the Lord's death until he comes". He only says "death" and does not add "Resurrection", although for him Christ's death would be "worthless" if he had not been raised (1 Cor 15:17). It is the perfect sacrifice of flesh and blood, hence the Cross, that is brought into the present. The entire First Letter is a journey from the Cross to the Resurrection; and the Eucharist, which is no triumphal feast, belongs on this journey, "for Christ our Passover has been sacrificed" (1 Cor 5:7). Whoever fails to heed the tremendous dignity, and hence the seriousness of this event, and is unable to "judge" how it differs from other meals, is "guilty of the body and the blood of the Lord" (11:27); "he . . . eats and drinks judgment to himself, if he does not judge the body rightly" (29). Here "the Body" can be understood not only as Christ's personal body but also as his Body, the Church, which is established through the Eucharist; thus lack of respect for the Lord's fellow members at the agape meal stands under the same threat of judgment. The judgment does not lie in Christ's sacrifice condemning us, but in our miscalculating the enormous distance between his sacrifice and our indifference. We are all "unworthy" (27) when we partake of the Eucharist, but it is precisely in underestimating this unworthiness that we pronounce our own judgment. Paul says this explicitly: "But if we judged ourselves rightly, we should not be judged" (31). Yet he does not look on this failure to judge ourselves as God's final word. He does not consider its harmful consequences (death and illnesses) as God's condemnation, but rather as the greater eucharistic love of the Lord disciplining and rebuking us (32)—which must not, however, allow us to fall back into irreverent carelessness again.

c. *Order.* It has already been stressed, that interpretation of the long section on spiritual gifts in Corinth (with its central chapter on love) has to begin with the conclusion, which contains its goal. Triggered by the lack of order at the worship service, the treatise uses two wide-ranging theological approaches to remedy the disorder. Chapter 12 discusses the purpose of spiritual gifts, which is to build up Christ's Body, the Church; chapter 13 elevates Christian love above even the most important spiritual gifts. Here Paul is exercising all his apostolic authority, as shown by his concluding statement: "But if anyone does not recognize this, he is not recognized" (1 Cor 14:38; cf. 7:40*b*, 11:16).

As he *begins to lay the foundation,* Paul lays the axe to the root of the Corinthians' spiritual arrogance. The very mention of being "led astray to the dumb idols" of the gentiles (12:2) is an indirect criticism of being similarly overwhelmed by something allegedly charismatic. Next comes the comment, that the Spirit leads to confessing Jesus as Lord (3), and that spiritual gifts are distributed not only by the Holy Spirit, but also by the Son and the Father, "who works all things in all", hence by the Trinity (4–6). The spiritual gifts, which are listed with no claim to system or completeness—different lists can be found in Romans 12 and Ephesians 4—derive their meaning and degree of importance from their service to the Body of Christ, whose various members work together in harmony for the sake of its unity. The expression "spiritual gift" is used in a completely open way here, just as it was in 7:7: Why should the permanent offices of the Church (specifically set apart in 12:28) not come at the beginning of the final list, which includes other gifts that are not offices in the same sense (28–29)? These, too, are ranked according to their usefulness to the Church, as indicated by the closing remark: "But earnestly desire the greater gifts" (31*a*). A detailed treatment of what determines the hierarchy is given in chapter 14.

The spiritual gifts, while basically distinct, are geared to the unity of the whole. But *love* surpasses all the "partial" gifts, which will pass away (13:10); this is stressed at the beginning of the chapter (13:1–2), and again in conclusion (13:8–10). If one asks which love is being described here, the answer is, of course, Christian love. Love of God and of one's neighbor are its inseparable components, but since the concern is to build up Christ's Body, the Church, love for our fellow man clearly takes precedence. Christ's own love, the characteristics of which are described in 13:4–7, could be taken as prototype: a love that does not seek its own, does not resent evil, that endures all things, and bears all things. When people try to live this kind of life, their love will not boast, will not be arrogant, will not rejoice in unrighteousness, et cetera. Taken together with the teaching on spiritual gifts, this means that if the individual gifts do not have love as their inner life's strength, they will be totally unable to carry out their service in building up the Church. The decisive confrontation between knowledge and love comes up again. No matter how high earthly knowledge is, no matter how absolute it fancies itself (even "full knowledge" of "all mysteries" [13:2]), it is always only "partial", it "will pass away" (9–10), and it remains nothing more than to "see in a mirror dimly" (12). Perfect understanding and absolute knowledge are not described as the personal possession of an infinite being, but as mutual recognition: knowing God in the same way he knows us, which is actually another form of love. The forms of earthly interpersonal love, faith, and hope reach their perfection as they enter into this perfect love (13).

Chapter 14 goes on to give detailed directions for worship services. Characteristically, it opens with another reference to love ("pursue love"), immediately followed by assigning superior rank to prophecy, that is, to interpreting unintelligible utterances in tongues, so that the congregation can understand them: "desire earnestly spiritual gifts, but especially that you may prophesy" (1 Cor 14:1). The only thing that really interests us today, in the long argument for valuing prophecy more than *glossolalia,* is one basic principle:

"Seek to abound for the edification of the Church" (14:12). Whatever fails to edify a participant in the service (17), and must even seem "mad" to an outsider, must absolutely be avoided. But it is also assumed that each member of the congregation can contribute something to benefit the service: "When you assemble, each one has a psalm, has a teaching, has a revelation, has a tongue, has an interpretation" (26). These examples were chosen to suit Corinthian conditions, but what remains valid for all time is the "active participation" of the entire congregation in the worship service, provided it centers on the importance and objective reality of the action of the eucharistic Lord.

IV

THE APOSTLE IN THE CONGREGATION

Everything up to this point has shown Paul set over against the congregation. He is God's fellow worker in building it up. He is more than its master instructor: he was the father who begot it. God qualified him in the Spirit to serve the New Covenant. The congregation is his laurel wreath, his letter of commendation; granted, he is not the author of the letter—Christ is—but he wrote it (2 Cor 3:3). Not only is the congregation on earth built on the foundation of the apostles (Eph 2:20), but the ultimate Church, the heavenly Jerusalem, also is built forever on the twelve foundation stones of the twelve apostles of the Lamb (Rev 21:14). John, Peter, and James, in their letters, also continue to be aware that they are sent as apostles, but this awareness is most strongly pronounced in Paul.

Yet he knows very well that even if he is not

a member of the individual congregation, he still is a member of the Church of Christ. That is repeatedly made clear in the letters to the Corinthians, in which his chief role, in replying to the congregation's questions, is to teach, scold, and encourage them. In these functions, also, he is always a mere servant who never for a moment takes himself for the Lord of the Church ("Paul was not crucified for you, was he?" [1 Cor 1:13]). He preaches "in weakness and in fear . . . that your faith should not rest on the wisdom of men, but on the power of God" (1 Cor 2:3, 5). What is more important: he refers to his office of apostle as just one of the spiritual gifts given by the Lord of the Church (1 Cor 12:28; cf. Eph 4:11), which still leaves a special place for the remaining offices.

But several passages make it clear that the Apostle places himself in the ranks of the faithful, so that he can receive God's gifts as they do. Sometimes the "we" of "God's fellow workers" is imperceptibly transformed into the "we" of all Christians. In 1 Corinthians 2, the "we" who proclaim the wisdom of God refers first to the apostles as a whole (in the broader sense); but when it is said (1 Cor 2:15) that he who is spiritual appraises all things, this applies to the mature Christian as well. A Pauline faction in the Church would be an inner contradiction (1 Cor 3:4). For him, as for everyone, Christ is "righteousness and sanctification and redemption" (1 Cor 1:30).

When he says, as though coining a proverb: "All things are lawful for me, but I will not be mastered by anything" (1 Cor 6:12), the "I" does not denote Paul but every Christian. And when he speaks of his celibacy (1 Cor 7:7), it is not really in order to set himself up as a model, but to encourage others to watch whether they are chosen for this by Christ. All the more, the "I" in the hymn of praise to love does not denote Paul; it is the "I" of every Christian who has grasped the central point of Christ's teaching, that "if I speak with the tongues of men and of angels . . . and know all mysteries . . . and have all faith . . . but do not have love, I am nothing" (1 Cor 13:1–3).

Probably the most striking point is made when, in the midst of describing the glory of the office of apostle, he imperceptibly switches to statements that undoubtedly apply to all serious Christians. First Paul compares the glory of Christian service with Moses' service in the Old Testament, but this connection already makes the "veil over the face of Moses" typical of all Israel: "But whenever a man turns to the Lord, the veil is taken away" (2 Cor 3:16). And this is even truer in the New Testament context: "But we all, beholding as in a mirror the glory of the Lord, are being transformed into the same image from glory to glory, just as from the Lord, the Spirit" (2 Cor 3:18). This "all" sets the whole congregation within the sphere of apostolic service, even though in the next verse (2 Cor 4:1) Paul returns to the "we" of the pastoral office ("therefore since we have this ministry, as we received mercy, we do not lose heart"). In the same connection, the apostolic "we" is just as clearly enlarged to include all Christians (in 2 Cor 5:1–10), when he describes the yearning expectation of believers on earth. As in the equivalent eighth chapter of Romans, this is true of Christianity as a whole, which lives by faith, not by sight, "absent" from its home and longing "to be at home with the Lord". Christianity as a whole is meant throughout. In 2 Corinthians 5:9, when Paul says, "Therefore also we have as our ambition, whether at home [in heaven] or absent [on earth], to be pleasing to him", the particular viewpoint of the Magisterium may chime in, but not as distinct from that of the congregation. The same is true again when the Christian teaching about the Resurrection is being defended: if Christ had not been raised, not just the apostles but all Christians would be "found to be false witnesses" (1 Cor 15:15). Christians are not merely hearers of the apostles' gospel; in everything he wrote, Paul expects them to be its representatives, in their own lives and in transmitting it, not just outwardly but in an inner communion of the saints, which Paul has grasped in the depths of his being (2 Cor 1:3–7; 1 Cor 12:14–26).

V

THE FINAL CONFRONTATION
(2 COR 10–13)

The Apostle's final wrestling with the difficult Corinthian congregation is recorded in the three last chapters of the Second Letter, revealing all the dimensions and tensions which a Christian dispute can manifest without breaking out of the framework of the Church. As was shown in the initial hypothesis, this closing portion was not written last, but is probably an excerpt from the "tearful letter", which was written between the First and Second letters, and was followed by the reconciliation (2 Cor 7:7). But there is a practical justification for the present order: this concluding passage contains the furthest limits that can be tolerated, theologically as well as in practice, in a struggle between the Magisterium and the congregation.

1. *Settling Accounts with the Accusers* (*2 Cor 10:1–8; 11:13–18*)

Paul uses unusually sharp language in answering those who—presumably during his intervening visit—accused him of unfitness to be an apostle, while the congregation remained silent on this point. He responds only to the key accusations, without going into his basic credentials again (his selection on the road to Damascus, cf. 1 Cor 9:1, and the hand of fellowship extended by the apostles in Jerusalem, cf. Gal 2:1–10). The wandering preachers who came with letters of recommendation (from Syria?) accused Paul chiefly of lacking experience in rhetoric, which made them doubt whether it was really "Christ who speaks in" him (2 Cor 13:3)—as well as of arrogance (10:12): he was "boasting beyond measure" (10:13, 15) in continually extending his mission territory (10:12–18). There might be another reproach as well, which had already started to make itself heard in the begging letter (2 Cor 8:20), if one interprets 2 Corinthians 12:16 as an accusation raised by the Corinthians: that he had misused the money that was collected, not by diverting some of it for himself but for his fellow workers.

There are two basic requirements for beginning to settle the accounts. The first is that he is to wage a war in the name of Christ—military images are used: "the destruction of fortresses, . . .

speculations, and every lofty thing raised up against the knowledge of God, and taking every thought captive to the obedience of Christ" (2 Cor 10:4–5)—but this battle will be waged solely with spiritual weapons, since others would not be "divinely powerful" enough to carry out the commission he has accepted. Twice he stresses that, in contrast to the authority given Jeremiah (Jer 1:10; 18:7), his authority was given only to build up, not to tear down (2 Cor 10:8; 13:10). In this he is a successor of Jesus, who could fight just as uncompromisingly with the spiritual sword of his word, but always in order to build up the Kingdom of God.

The second prerequisite for settling the accounts is found in 2 Corinthians 10:6: "We are ready to punish all disobedience, whenever your obedience is complete." This is important. Paul is not entering into single combat against enemies in the congregation, while its members neutrally observe a sporting match. He starts the fight only when he is sure of the congregation, just as he undertook official actions only when he was sure of their spiritual consent. Here their complete obedience is starkly contrasted with the disobedience that will be punished.

With this precondition he begins his attack, which continues as far as chapter 13. The reproach leveled against him was that in letters and from afar he could be "weighty and strong" (10:10) "but in person he is unimpressive and his speaking amounts to nothing." The answer is brief; its full scope is not revealed until the thirteenth chapter: "Such people should realize that what we are in our letters when we are absent, we will be in our actions when we are present" (10:11). This contains—not for the first or the last time—a warning meant to be taken very seriously: "What do you desire? Shall I come to you with a rod or with love and a spirit of gentleness?" (1 Cor 4:21). In the final confrontation the warning is even sharper: "If I come again, I will not spare anyone" (2 Cor 13:2). We will be occupied with the scope of this threat in the closing show of force. Suffice it for now that he uses this warning to parry the scorn of those opponents claiming superiority, whom he dubs "super-apostles" (11:5; 12:11). Paul does not even consider defending himself against the charge of lacking the rhetoric which was so prized in those times. In the context of all his letters, this apparent or genuine weakness ("I was with you in weakness and in fear and in much trembling", 1 Cor 2:3) certainly has a theological rather than a psychological basis: the Apostle was not permitted to come with "persuasive words of wisdom ... that your faith should not rest on the wisdom of men, but on the power of God" (1 Cor 2:4–5). In the final round he will state it thus: "Power is perfected in weakness" (2 Cor 12:9), "for we also are weak in him [Christ], yet we shall live with him because of the power of God directed toward you" (13:4). This shows to what extent Paul meets his opponents with purely spiritual weapons.

The other reproach against which he must defend himself is that of *arrogance* and a desire for fame. The Apostle immediately turns this weapon against his attackers: "We are not so bold to class or compare ourselves with some of those who commend themselves" (2 Cor 10:12, alluding to the letters of commendation that his opponents brought with them), "for not he who commends himself is approved, but whom the Lord commends" (10:18). This points back to Paul's apostolic success with the Corinthians: they are his "letters of commendation" written by the Lord (2 Cor 3:1ff.). If the Corinthians are his fame (and he theirs in the day of the Lord Jesus [2 Cor 1:14]), then the Apostle is not overextending himself, since he limits himself to precisely the measure of ministry to the gentiles to which he was appointed by God and the original apostles (10:13–14). Neither does he intrude on areas in which others have labored (10:16), which is just what his opponents, who intruded into Corinth, are doing. And since the territory of the gentiles extends further than Corinth, he can, without arrogance, express the hope that he will advance still further (perhaps to Rome).

He has more arguments to show that he measures his activity by the task he has been given and not, like his opponents, "by themselves" (10:12). In the first place, he made no claims of his own on the congregation but instead made it the goal of all his zeal that, like a modest best man, "I might present you as a pure virgin" to Christ (11:2). But he does express concern, in the same words as in the Letter to the Galatians, that this bride might be diverted from the true gospel by the serpent's cunning, as Eve was. "When someone comes preaching another Jesus than the one we preached, or when you receive a different spirit than the one you received [from my preaching] . . . you seem to endure it quite well" (11:4; cf. Gal 1:6–9).

Now the opponents can be exposed on the spot as "false apostles, deceitful workers" (11:13) and thus as "servants of Satan", since it is well known that he can disguise himself as an angel of light. Paul predicts a fitting end for them. This reminds one more of the exorcisms of Jesus than of Paul's excommunications, always aimed at healing. We are dealing here with a curse (analogous to that against the infiltrators in Galatia). Paul may truly ask: "What fellowship has light with darkness? Or what harmony has Christ with Belial?" (2 Cor 6:14–15).

The foolishness of God is true wisdom, and it is just this paradox that now leads the Apostle to deliver his great "foolish" speech, in which he carries the reproach of self-glorification *ad ab-*

surdum and uses the pastoral office's lot to illustrate once again the paradox of Christian existence.

2. *The Paradox of Life in Office (2 Cor 11:16–12:11a)*

The speech which now follows has a strange introduction. Paul is going to boast; he needs the congregation's permission to speak foolishly for once despite his wisdom ("let no one think me foolish" [11:16]). And he contrasts his foolishness with the way the Lord would speak (17). This means he will not place his speech on the same level as the foolishness of God, which manifested itself in the Cross of Christ. He gives a sarcastic reason: "For you, being so wise, bear with the foolish gladly", which is drastically elaborated: you bear with every form of exploitation and humiliation by the super-apostles—"we have been weak by comparison!" (19–21a).

Here begins the paradoxical "rhetoric" he uses to describe a truly apostolic existence. It has two distinct parts. The first depicts the earthly hardships of this kind of life: they are the marks of its authenticity, because they are direct proof that such a life follows the example of Christ (11:22–23). The second part is different; its heights and depths are not of this earth. This life moves between heaven and hell: first caught up into paradise and then buffeted by a thorn in the flesh, a messenger of Satan—till at last he can reach the conclusion that "Power is perfected in weakness" (12:9).

The first part sweeps aside the intruders' boasts about being descendants of Abraham: he is their equal in this regard (11:22). But he is not on the same level with them when it comes to being "servants of Christ". Now (always speaking foolishly) he begins proving his superiority, point by point. He lists the hardships and abuse, the dangers threatening on all sides, and in addition to this external suffering, the extent of internal distress that overburdens him daily, since he is not only unable to resist the pressure but also to suffer with all who experience weakness and to bleed with each case of backsliding. All this is a new and final proof for the Corinthians that a true apostle shows himself as such by bearing his cross each day, as the Lord predicted in Damascus, when he said: "I will show him how much he must suffer for my name's sake" (Acts 9:16). Already in this first section, the conclusion is a paradox: "If I have to boast, I will boast of what pertains to my weakness" (11:30).

The full scope, however, is only revealed in *the second part*. When Paul begins telling about his visions, he shrouds himself in anonymity ("I know a man" [12:2]), but leaves no doubt that he himself is that man. He is not interested in describing the subjective nature of the ecstasy ("whether in the body . . . or out of the body"

[12:3]), but of his objective experience; he explicitly states that the words he heard were "inexpressible" and that man was unable or "not permitted" to speak them. This sentence should not be interpreted in a framework of non-Christian mysticism but within the revelation of Jesus Christ, which is a revelation of the Word. Of course this Word has infinite depths, even when seen through human eyes and preached by the Church. These are revealed to certain believers at God's pleasure, so that their human utterances will be impregnated with its immeasurable riches. We never know all there is to be known because infinite love exceeds the limits of all finite knowledge, as Paul himself stated (Eph 3:19). Hiding himself in anonymity permits Paul to praise this man who was so blessed, and to distinguish him from himself, who wants to boast only about his weaknesses (12:5–6). To guard against any vainglory, the one who received a foretaste of heaven must now become acquainted with a spirit of hell, which is so unendurable that when it buffets him he can do nothing but beg God to end the torment. He begs in vain. For "my grace", which is to be "sufficient" for the man led through heaven and hell, allows him, as a follower of the Lord, to experience both conditions again: being united with God and being abandoned by him, which can be truly felt only by one who has known him before.

The concluding axiom, "Power is perfected in

weakness" (12:9–10) is, as 13:3–4 shows, to be interpreted solely on the foundation of Christology. It is also the theme whose variations make up the final portion of the letter.

First Paul sharply concludes the settling of accounts with his opponents and the paradoxical proofs of his own authority. Here, and in what follows, one can see that the "complete obedience" (10:6) he demands of the congregation is not yet simply taken for granted; the sharp, sometimes reproachful tone with which he addresses the congregation, continues to the end. They "compelled" him to his foolish speech. "Actually I should have been commended by you" and defended against the super-apostles, "for in no respect was I inferior to the super-apostles, even though I am nobody"—yes, precisely because I am nobody! (12:11). And as though casually, in a postscript, he points to a new proof of his authority: "with all perseverance" Paul performed "signs and wonders and miracles" in Corinth (12:12). He makes no great thing of it, less than Luke does in his Acts of the Apostles, when he tells how Peter and Paul healed the sick and raised the dead. Instead he immediately turns to the topic that recurs so frequently: that he did not become a burden to the congregation and that he is not interested in their possessions but only in themselves, in contrast to normal custom, "for children are not obliged to save up for their parents, but parents for their children" (12:14). But the more love the Apostle has poured out upon the congregation, the less he seems to be loved by them in return. Are they really going to reproach him with having impure motives concerning the money that was donated? Or if he did not exploit them himself, did Titus "take any advantage of you"? (12:14–18). The more the problems of the forthcoming third visit (12:14) present themselves concretely in his spirit, the more the Apostle's tone grows somber. We must bear in mind that when he wrote these chapters, he had not yet received the comforting news which Titus brought back from Corinth. So the Apostle girds his loins for the last round of the battle, no longer just with individual opponents but with the congregation as a whole. This final round also brings the climax of Paul's pastoral message.

3. *The Final Round (2 Cor 12:19–13:13)*

First, the situation must be realistically evaluated. What was just said—that he made short work of his opponents, and the description of following the Cross—will presumably be misunderstood as self-defense. But Paul spoke "in the sight of God ... in Christ" and, once again, not in order to tear down but only to build up the congregation (12:19). He was only doing his duty. But how can this be understood by a people whom he left in such disorder at his interim visit? He is afraid that when he comes again he will find the same deplorable state of affairs and so "God may humiliate me before you" (21). So he paints the Corinthians a detailed picture of their sins. In doing so, he goes back to what he reproached them with in the First Letter and adds to that the things he experienced during his interim visit. The list gets long, but there is certainly nothing in it that is not justified. "For I am afraid that perhaps when I come . . . there may be strife, jealousy, angry tempers, disputes, slanders, gossip, arrogance, disturbances" (20), and that back of these Christian vices, the old paganism of these supposed converts may still lie hidden—"impurity, immorality, and sensuality" (21)—perhaps under the cloak of charismatic freedom.

All this must at all cost be rooted out by Paul on his next visit. What means should he use? Loving-kindness, patience, and signs and wonders (12:12) did not bear fruit. So finally the full authority of his office must be exercised, provoked not only by the sinfulness of the congregation, but by their literally "seeking for proof of the Christ who speaks", in his power, in Paul (13:3). But it is just this power of Christ that is Paul's full authority. He produces it and holds it up before them: "I have previously said when present the second time, and though now absent I say in advance to those who have sinned in the past and to all the rest as well, that if I come again, I will not spare anyone" (13:2). You are bringing this on yourselves.

Paul in no way sets the authority of his office in opposition to his love for the congregation. But if there is no other way, this love can assume the character they were warned about. Why? Because the harmony he called for between his full loving authority and the loving obedience of the congregation (10:6) no longer exists. But is such a condition even possible in Christ's Church? Threatening to use the authority of his office is not unchristian because that authority is not separate from Paul's love. But can it be Christian to carry out the threat if love no longer rules the other side? One is reminded of the analogous situation in the First Letter: "Now some have become arrogant, as though I were not coming to you. But I will come to you soon, if the Lord wills, and I shall find out, not the words of those who are arrogant, but their power. For the kingdom of God does not consist in words, but in power. What do you desire? Shall I come to you with a rod or with love and a spirit of gentleness?" (1 Cor 4:18–21). The authority of the Church contains no contradiction to the godly love which appeared in Christ. The contradiction is only in the person who contradicts it. "Knowledge puffs up, but love [alone] edifies" (1 Cor 8:1). Paul fights only with spiritual weapons, and these "are not of the flesh, but divinely powerful" (2 Cor 10:4). But when they encounter purely fleshly opposition, they can only operate mercilessly. In other words, when a person opposes the Church's love, which incorporates the authority of Christ, that person is found guilty of having excommunicated himself from love and from communion.

Is this to be the end? Not for Paul. But now he can only return to the wellspring of the Church's authority, to the crucified and risen Lord. If the Corinthians want to find out for themselves whether Christ is speaking through Paul, he takes this as reason for tying together three (typically Pauline) statements:

1. Christ is not weak toward you but strong in you.
2. "He was crucified because of weakness, yet he lives because of the power of God" (13:4).
3. We also are weak in him, yet we shall show ourselves alive with him in facing you, because of the power of God.

The first statement presupposes the second: from the strength of him who was crucified and rose again, the Church is strong in herself, whether she wants to be or not. Christ is objectively strong in Corinth; it is not as one who is weak and crucified that he confronts them (and their own supposed strength). Paul will come back to this first statement later, as he makes a decisive pastoral move (13:5). The second sentence shows that in the Church and her history, the impotence of the Cross does not operate separately from the power of the Resurrection. The ongoing immediacy of the Cross is a grace given to the Church by the resurrected Christ, who is seated on high. This is especially true of the authority of the pastoral office: Peter is given the authority together with the prediction of his crucifixion. Paul (as he has repeatedly shown in both letters) experiences his life as one who is crucified, both in weakness and in being gifted with the strength of the risen Christ. Thus the difference shown earlier (at 2 Cor 4:10–12) becomes apparent again, between the Cross and Resurrection of Christ and Paul's cross (conferred as grace by Christ's Resurrection). As far as the congregation with its purely human weakness is concerned, it is only promised Christ's strength; its faults have nothing to do with the weakness of the Cross. But what this analysis reveals about the Apostle's actual situation is that, despite or rather because of his weakness, he will be able to show himself to the congregation as living and powerful, from God's strength rather than from his own.

And now comes the application that surprises the Corinthians and yet follows directly from the first statement: "Test yourselves to see if you are in the faith; examine yourselves (*dokimazein*). Or do you not recognize this about yourselves (and are you incapable of recognizing), that Jesus Christ is in you?" (13:5) None of the accusations against the Apostle could have been made if this self-examination and recognition had occurred. For indeed Christ *is* in the congregation, in the unity of Cross and Resurrection, and thus also of obedience and love. For his "becoming obedient to the point of death, even death on a cross" is certain proof of God's triune love for the world, a love embodied in the Church as the Body of Christ. The family of words *"dokimazein-dokimē-dokimos"* (to test, to prove, approved or genuine) dominates the verses that follow. The Corinthians would only have been approved if self-examination had brought them to recognize that Christ dwells in the congregation, so that they could judge the Apostle with the mind of Christ. If they failed to understand this, then they would "fail the test" (13:5). If they were approved, they would have to recognize Paul's being approved precisely in the paradox of his weakness: "But I trust that you will realize that we ourselves do not fail the test" (6). He not only trusts it is so, he also prays that the congregation will do what is right ("that you do no wrong" [7]), because it has recognized the spirit of Christ in itself.

And now Paul closes the verse with an astonishing and wonderful expression: "even though we should appear unapproved". For he is praying "not that we ourselves may appear approved", but rather to gain approval for the congregation, if need be at the cost of appearing unapproved himself. For actually this is just what he has always found to be true: not only that the Apostle must come last and the congregation first (1 Cor 4:9)—that was said ironically—but that "death works in us, but life in you" (2 Cor 4:12), which is a simple description of the work assigned to the Apostle and to the pastoral office as a whole. "For we can do nothing against the truth [of the Cross], but only for the truth" (13:8). And so in the end, the crucifixion of and low opinion of the pastoral office appear as only right and proper: "For we rejoice when we ourselves are weak but you are strong; this we also pray for, that you be made complete" (13:9). Paul does not go on to explain what this consists of—but undoubtedly not in holding the pastoral office in low esteem, but rather in the deeper insight that its weakness denotes its being crucified with Christ for the benefit of the Church.

Thus in closing it is again demonstrated, that the warning Paul gave from afar while absent, proves unnecessary "when [I am] present", because the reconciliation, which a proper understanding of the Church calls for, has already taken place. Therefore it can be stressed again, that the

New Testament "authority which the Lord gave", even when it occasionally must issue a warning, is "for building up and not for tearing down" (13:10).

Leaving all polemic behind, the conclusion is formulated purely in terms of Church harmony: "Finally brethren, rejoice, be made complete, be comforted, be like-minded, live in peace; and the God of love and peace shall be with you" (13:11). So you will truly become what objectively you already are. The liturgical holy kiss shall set the seal on this, greetings from other congregations shall strengthen it, and the Apostle's benediction can impart to the congregation the grace of the Trinity: the love of the Father and the Son, in which they are enfolded by the Holy Spirit. (12–14).

> "The grace of the Lord Jesus Christ,
> and the love of God,
> and the fellowship of the Holy Spirit,
> be with you all."